650 | Siblings

Edited by Edward McCann

650 | WHERE WRITERS READ
Founder / Editor • Edward McCann
Executive Producer • Richard Kollath
Literary Ombudsman • Steven Lewis
Director of Operations • Jane Kaupp
Design Director • Diane Fokas
Social Media Strategist • Shayna Miller
Director of Photography • Kevin O'Connor
Chief Audio Engineer • Jesse Chason
Videography / Photography • Sara Caldwell
Copy Editor • Shelley Sadler Kenney
Technical Advisor • Conrad Trautmann
Technical Advisor • Stephen Kaupp

Production Assistants
Robert Dennison, Lynn Dennison, Mackenzie Meeks,
Jackie Mercurio, Brian Reagher, and Isabella Fokas

Advisory Committee
Rachel Aydt, Laura Shaine Cunningham, Angela Davis-Gardner,
Karen Dukess, Joseph Goodrich, David Masello, Honor Molloy,
Irene O'Garden, John Pielmeier, Gretchen Reed, James Russek,
Angela Derecas Taylor, and Julie Trelstad

"It snowed last year too: I made a snowman and my brother knocked it down and then I knocked my brother down and then we had tea."

—*Dylan Thomas*

ABOUT 650

They are our best friends and they are our worst enemies. They are nature's way of creating a different version of ourselves. They are our confidants, our companions, and our playmates, and they know us better than anyone. Love them or hate them, our relationships with our siblings are likely the longest relationships we will have with anyone, ever. The dozen stories we've assembled here reflect a broad range of sibling experiences.

650 is a celebration of writing and the spoken word, a literary forum for personal stories performed five minutes—and 650 words—at a time. Our events at theaters, colleges, and libraries around the country are organized around single, broad topics that invite a range of expression, and recorded performances are added to a digital archive of writers reading their work aloud. The writers and their work receive additional exposure through podcasts, broadcasts, our YouTube channel, and in these printed volumes. The stories collected here were first performed for a live audience at Nancy Manocherian's *the cell* in New York City.

650 features graduate students and grandparents, first-timers and best-selling writers. It's all about the writing, with an emphasis on craft. It's about the choice of one word over another, about the shape of sentences and paragraphs, the arc of a narrative, the poetry of a unique literary voice. If you love language and enjoy a good story, you've come to the right place. To submit your work or attend our shows, visit our website or Facebook page, and join our mailing list.

Please tell your friends about 650, and spread the word about the spoken word.

Ed McCann

Edward McCann, Founder / Editor

READ650.COM
FACEBOOK.COM/READ650

CONTENTS

My Dadashi • Rahimeh Andalibian / 1

The Crime on the Catechism • Irene O'Garden / 5

B-flat • Mary Catherine Bolster / 9

With Or Without You • Ann Casapini / 13

First Love • Betty MacDonald / 17

The Ruination of Everything • Steven Lewis / 21

The Last Time • Julie Evans / 25

Beat the Reaper • Stephen J. Brown / 29

Witnesses • John Gredler / 33

Kodachrome • Ann Levin / 37

Connected • Jackie Mercurio / 41

Rotten Little Liars • Edward McCann / 45

Acknowledgments / 57

Edited by Edward McCann

RAHIMEH ANDALIBIAN

Dr. Rahimeh Andalibian is a psychologist and the author of the memoir, *The Rose Hotel*, which has received a starred review from *Publisher's Weekly* and topped Amazon's number one bestseller list in the memoir category. "Dr. A" self-published the book and on its one-year anniversary, *The Rose Hotel* was sold to National Geographic and was re-released in 2015. The book chronicles the story of her Iranian Muslim family and their fight to survive after a tragedy destroys the idyllic life they once led in the Holy City of Mashhad (second only to Mecca). Their peaceful life in their own luxury hotel ends and they are uprooted and exiled to London, then to California. Dr. Andalibian works as a licensed clinical psychologist in New York City specializing in family therapy, trauma, spectrum issues, and business coaching with social entrepreneurs.

MY DADASHI

Rahimeh Andalibian

I was the only girl in a family of boys, three older brothers. Then my mother became pregnant again in the hope of giving me a baby sister. Before the birth, my parents bought the unborn baby and me girl-to-be matching tiny golden earrings. I ended up with two sets of earrings; the baby was another boy.

After baby Iman's birth, my mother had her tubes tied. There would be no more attempts for a baby sister. In secret, I always gloated that Iman had not been another girl, but my own personal baby toy, sweet and peaceful as a little Buddha. He was always trailing after me, sucking candies and calling for me, as he would for my mother in a babyish combination of our names, "Maman Rahimeh!"

We grew up in a house on the grounds of the hotel my father had built—The Rose Hotel, the second largest hotel in Mashhad Iran, which catered to religious pilgrims visiting the great golden-domed mosque next door. After Mecca, this mosque was the most sacred destination in the world for the Shiite Muslims. The hotel advertised "No Alcohol, No Music, No Women in Immodest Dress," which was

1

a big draw in the Mid-East.

For me and Iman, The Rose Hotel was also the fantasy playground of all time. All our young lives, we dreamed of running wild through its rooms and hallways. But we were always watched until one day, mysteriously, I led my little brother inside the hotel and found—to our delight—it was deserted. Along with the guests, the staff had vanished—the doorman in his brown jacket with the gold buttons; the maids in their crisp white uniforms. No one to shout, "Stop! You are not allowed in there." We could run, climb balustrades, and peek into the forbidden chambers.

As we ran through the marble halls, we paused to filch refreshments at the tea and reception room. We found the pistachio nougat candies hidden in the pantry, intended as treats for guests, and then made the most magnificent discovery in the fridge: Akbar-Mashdi ice cream! We licked our lips like kittens, and then tiptoed past the prayer room overseen by the portrait of Imam Ali, the son-in-law of Prophet Mohammad. His stern visage, topped in black headdress, glowered, as if he could see our misdeeds.

We were not chasened for long. We aimed for the summit, the top floor crystal banquet room.

Iman took my hand and we entered. I felt my heart beat faster. We dragged ten of the tables together, put dishes over the cleared tabletops, and placed silverware in lines, creating highways and streets. Our giggles echoed through the deserted hotel, the single sound. For hours, we played in our make-believe city. Then suddenly, not far away, I heard men yelling. I was too young to understand their words: "revolution," "rape," and "execution." But I knew something frightening had begun. I grabbed Iman's hand and pushed us down to duck behind the heavy tapestry hanging on the main lobby's wall— "Hide!"

We could hear men running through the hotel. Someone paused, stopped. I could feel him—a heaving presence on the other side of the wall hanging.

I held my breath. "Shhh . . . " I whispered to Iman. But it was too late. He let out a baby squeak of fear.

A big hand pushed open the tapestry. I looked into dark, burning eyes, magnified by black-rimmed eyeglasses—our father, Baba. "Aha!"

There was no time to scold us. "Quick, run ... into the house!"

Baba watched us cross the lawn to our home sequestered within the grounds of the hotel.

From outside, we heard the sounds of chanting and breaking glass. I held Iman to my chest. It was 1979 and the Revolution had overtaken us. I was four years old and Iman was two. Soon we would have to leave Iran and say goodbye to the Rose Hotel forever, but then, all that mattered was that I could feel my brother's small heart beat against mine.

IRENE O'GARDEN

Irene O'Garden has won or been nominated for prizes in nearly every writing category from stage to e-screen, hardcovers, as well as literary magazines and anthologies. Her critically-acclaimed play, *Women On Fire*, played sold-out houses at Off-Broadway's Cherry Lane Theatre and was nominated for a Lucille Lortel Award. O'Garden won a Pushcart Prize for her lyric essay *"Glad To Be Human,"* and HarperCollins published her first memoir *Fat Girl.: One Woman's Way Out*. O'Garden's second memoir, *Risking the Rapids: How My Wilderness Journey Healed my Childhood*, was recently published by Mango. O'Garden's work has been featured in dozens of literary journals and anthologies. *Fulcrum*, published by Nirala, is her first poetry collection. She is joyfully married to writer John Pielmeier.

4

THE CRIME ON THE CATECHISM

Irene O'Garden

I was born in the middle. In the middle of seven children, in a mid-size city in the middle of the country, in the middle class, in the middle of the twentieth century. Our youngest sibling, my only baby sister: Ro for Rosemary. This little girl Ro does not ask for much: to be tossed in the air by her father (though she's too old) to tell the best joke at the table, to be absorbed in something long enough to get good at it and then forget she's good at it and just do it. For her, that is drawing.

Take this finger, she thinks, staring at it in class one day. Maybe I could draw so well people couldn't tell it's a drawing.

She pencils a careful sketch on the grocery-bag cover she made to protect her catechism. Funny baggy knuckle, curved fingertip, hint of fingernail.

Not every finger, just the one. One like her, in a twitching hand of siblings.

She shades the sides. The instant she thinks, "I might be good at this," her teacher roars, "What does this mean?!" and yanks the book away.

Ro is bewildered. "What?"

"You know! Obscenity! Obscenity!"

Oh. But only years later, does Ro, realize: She gave the catechism "the finger."

The teacher grips Ro's arm as deep as a dog bite. Next day, five blue oval fingertip bruises will surface.

Mouth dry, spinning with shock, Ro is marched over the unyielding terrazzo, through the wood and starry glass door into the principal's office.

"Call her parents immediately. I won't have her in my class!"

The call is made; Ro is sent home.

The artist does not understand her crime. Nor does Dad that night. He inspects the catechism.

"What were you drawing, honey?"

She holds up her left index finger. Gives Dad—in all innocence—"the finger."

"What did I do wrong, Dad?"

"Your teacher has a sick mind. She thinks it's a vulgar gesture."

He calls Monsignor Colbert. At this time of night. I hear the buzz and murmur of his explanation, then his accelerating professional Broadcaster thunder (my father is the Voice of … Montgomery Ward.

"That drawing is perfectly innocent. This warped woman is libelling my daughter. If there's one black mark on her record, I will sue the teacher, I will sue the school and I will sue the Catholic Church if need be."

Mom turns whiter than her usual pallor with embarrassment, yet she too knows her daughter is innocent. Her eldest child, a daughter—is a NUN. This baby daughter is a child who used to ask permission every night to sing herself to sleep.

The school capitulates.

As for the girl? The teacher's shriek, the public humiliation, the chill of the principal's office, her mother's gasp, her father's fury, her own molten confusion flowed into the muscles of her arm and hardened into doubt. Her drawings become tinier and tinier. Unquestionably non controversial. Never again "the finger." Though one horn—a Unicorn. Daisies. Valentines. An artist exiled from anatomy.

MARY CATHERINE BOLSTER

Mary Catherine Bolster grew up in Iowa but not on a farm. She has been writing in one form or another since her first feature column in *The Compass*, her high school paper. She holds advanced degrees in nursing and medical ethics and began her career on the clinical faculty of the University of Iowa. Mary Catherine published articles in *Linacre Quarterly* and other medical/ethical journals before writing consumer-oriented articles for regional consumer magazines and national trade publications as a freelancer. The company she founded—MCB Communications—served health care and nonprofit clients, specializing in capital campaigns, consumer and medical writing, and public relations. She currently lives in Manhattan and from time to time yearns for her beloved prairie.

B-FLAT

Mary Catherine Bolster

Growing up in 1950s Iowa, my sister Beverly, seven years older, was my de facto mother. It was Beverly who sustained me through childhood tragedies like my beloved parakeet's death when I was seven. Took the sting out of a grade school bully's cruel words. Taught me how to make doll clothes from pastel flannel and satin ribbons while sitting on her big double bed.

And when I mastered playing piano, we made music together. I would accompany her strong soprano voice: opera arias, Broadway tunes, church hymns.

After she married and moved to Cedar Rapids, I married too but I didn't stay in Iowa. I moved a thousand miles away to Philadelphia.

Time, careers, petty jealousies, and foolish misunderstandings eventually replaced our harmonies with silence. I watched from a distance, as sips of wine became her solace against the discordance of everyday life.

Eventually Beverly stopped singing. Not in a church choir. Nor a local a capella group. Nothing.

And then—the dementia.

My sister died last year. Beverly was seventy-five.

On the subway platform, the B train rolls to a stop at 81st Street. I step into the crowded, hot car. I'm overdressed, can't move my arms to loosen my wool scarf. No ear buds to create a music bubble. No cell service to check Hop Stop. Can't see the transit map and can't move anyway amidst this throng of no-eye-contact, stone-faced New Yorkers.

Why this journey? To see a vocal coach of all things. My new shrink, who I sought out in a last-ditch attempt to find out why I'm still so angry with my dear, departed sister, said: "Performing makes you feel heard. Connected. So do it."

I found Jean through the *Open Center* catalog. Sixty-ish, thin as a rail, graceful, articulate, classically trained. She thinks I've got talent—should begin auditioning again. Really Jean. I'm almost 70.

For half the lesson, she softens my rigid body using precise Alexander Technique cues, her fingertips barely touching my torso, my diaphragm freer with each breath. After a warm-up, I sing Sondheim or Jerry Herman or eighteenth century solos in Italian. Somehow my voice seems clearer, lighter. I'm lighter. For that one hour each week, there's nothing in the world but music. Something to purge this anger.

After the session, I rush out to get to the Fulton Street station with five minutes to spare. Above the hum of the morning commute, I hear what sounds like organ and harp music coming from terminal lobby. I walk up just as a lone violinist begins to play Gounod's Ave Maria.

My sister and I loved this piece of music, this gem, a masterful combination of a much-loved Bach prelude and the soulful melody Gounod added years later. It was always a crowd-pleaser when we performed it for family gatherings, or local weddings, and High Mass at St. Joseph's.

I lean against a steel pillar in the morning light to listen and remember a summer day when we were performing this piece in a clapboard country church, shutters opened to the surrounding green fields. Beverly's voice perfectly suited for the melody's range, filling every corner.

I stay there, transported, slipping on my Ray-Bans to conceal the tears. I am the sole audience for this pop-up performance.

My train comes and goes. But I do not walk away, I cannot. Not until the violinist plays the last, luxurious B-flat.

ANN CASAPINI

Ann Casapini's most recent short piece on 'Perseverance' was published in the December 2016 issue of *The Sun*. She received an Honorable Mention in the *Westchester Review*'s recent 2016 Flash Fiction contest, and she's had two non-fiction pieces published in the online literary journal, *The Intima, A Journal of Narrative Medicine*. She studies writing with Steve Lewis at the Sarah Lawrence College Writing Institute. Ann has been a yoga and meditation practitioner and teacher for twenty years. She is also a singer and recently recorded songs for the short film *"Red Thread: The Prisoner and the Painter."* Ann lives with her husband, son, and dog in Tuckahoe, New York.

WITH OR WITHOUT YOU

Ann Casapini

I'm wearing headphones, pacing in circles on the dirt
driveway, blasting the U2 song "With or Without You," tears falling
off my face. I am exercising my brother's soon-to-be-orphaned dog,
Maggie. She knows something is terribly wrong and walks with
her tail down. My brother is inside his small apartment, making
a frantic attempt to pack up all his stuff. Our mother is inside
helping.

See the stone set in your eyes, See the thorn twist in your side, I
wait for you.

My brother's eyes are usually a beautiful green, but today
they look gray and hard like slate. He hasn't slept in forty-eight
hours, not since the police searched his place. At moments he's
hyper, talking non-stop and considering escaping to Canada or
Mexico. Then he becomes withdrawn and seems in a trance.

I am walking around and around. The September sun is still
burning hot. I want to vomit. I crank up the music to drown out my

thoughts.

With or without you, With or without you

But I keep hearing my brother's phone call to me two days before.

"I may have killed someone," he says.

No! Not you, my baby brother.

I taught you how to read! We used to sit in the dogwood tree together! You would never do this.

"Is your girlfriend alright?" I blurt out.

"Yes ... But she betrayed me. I sent him a letter bomb."

"What?"

Now I am bargaining with God. Please make this not true. Make it so no one was hurt. Make my brother all right. Was he drinking? Did he black-out? Is he bipolar?

I am pacing the driveway, guarding against flashing lights.

And you give yourself away, And you give yourself away

As if it were an ordinary day, we load boxes into the car. As if it were an ordinary day, we go to a café for lunch. As if it were any ordinary day, we say "please" and "thank you." And when dessert arrives, I think they've brought it to the wrong table because there's a candle on it. But my brother reminds me it's my thirty-second birthday and I start to cry again.

As we drive along Main Street on our way to a lawyer's office, I notice we're being followed by a police car. My armpits are wet. Was I speeding? Are they coming after my brother already? But after a few turns, they stop following us. I don't know why.

My head hurts. I want to help my brother. I want to damn him. I want to cradle him. I want to slap him.

What can I do?

And the money? No one in our family can afford a big defense.

The attorney's reception area is so quiet, I hear my heart pounding.

When the lawyer comes out to meet us, I want to fall on my knees and scream and beg this stranger to save my brother from his fate, but I am silent as they walk into his office. My mother and I sit like statues. After forty-five minutes, the lawyer asks us all to wait in the library. The only sound is the clock ticking.

And you give yourself away. And you give yourself away.

The large oak front door opens and four armed Federal Marshals enter.

They read my brother his Miranda rights. Sobbing, I hold him tight one last time.

They handcuff him and shackle my brother's feet.

They walk him outside to their car, shove him into the back seat.

They slam the door shut and drive away.

BETTY MacDONALD

Writer/actor **Betty MacDonald** contributed to the writing of and performed in TMI's *What To Expect When You're Not Expecting*. Her essay *Before Roe v Wade* appears in the anthology *Get Out of My Crotch*, published by Cherry Bomb Press. Betty especially enjoys reading aloud and frequently reads her work at spoken word events throughout the Hudson River Valley. Following her early career as a continuity writer and radio personality, Betty freelanced for many years as a travel writer. For the last twenty-six years, storytelling has influenced her work as a performer with Community Playback Theatre, a regional improvisational acting company. Her memoir, *Basking In The Glow Of Her Golden Years*, is nearly complete.

FIRST LOVE

Betty MacDonald

Because he slips into her bed at night after he comes home from a date. Because he is insistent, she lets him. She lets him because she adores her brother with the intensity of a little sister. She knows it's wrong.

She longs for his approval. After years of ignoring her and putting her down, he's focused on her. He wants her. She wants to be special.

She tries to stop but the lure to please him overrides her resistance.

She stops him from "going all the way." They do everything else. Her boundaries battered and porous from her father's incessant assault ... she wonders if her brother is also the object of unwanted touching from their father.

When she is nine and her brother thirteen, they are the same height. Their mother's nightmare: a shrimp of a son and a giant daughter. At eleven and fifteen, they look like twins, twin nymphs. He is tall by then and handsome. They're so young, so fresh bodied, like star crossed lovers … like loving brother and sister god and goddess in a Greek myth … in a Celtic myth … in a Viking myth. So much alike, could you tell them apart when they were entwined in each other's arms?

On a visit to their uncle a few years later, their uncle remarks, "You act as if you are his wife, not his sister."

Is that just a snarky remark? Does he know?

Does he know her fantasy dream-like locked away secret, not to be revealed, not to be acted upon: Her lover, a male version of herself, her exact counterpart. No one can know.

Fortunately what they share is forbidden. Without that inhibition, she would have lost herself in him.

On the one hand, she is dragged down by the weight of the secret … the forbidden-ness of it.

On the other, she loves their star crossedness, love-that-can-never-be, tragic story of it. Willingly, she promises herself she will welcome letting go when he commits to someone else.

When it ends, it has gone on for ten years.

They never speak about it. They don't even have a name for it. Later on she tells friends, therapists, a twelve-step group, anyone who will listen. He tells no one. He doesn't admit it to himself.

In his early sixties, he is diagnosed with Alzheimer's. When she visits him at his nursing home, he thinks it is 1950, and that they are in their teens.

On these rare visits, they sit side by side, holding hands, saying little. She could say she feels their souls touching, she could say there is an electric current, but it's not like that. A powerful feeling like no other courses from his hand into hers. She weeps whenever she remembers the feeling of their hands pressed together.

He was mean when they were kids. He never forgave her for reducing his lofty privileged only-child status to that of big brother. She had loved him unconditionally, in spite of his cutting her hair off, sawing her tricycle in half, burning the end of her nose with the cigarette lighter in the new Chevrolet. Her cousin asks, "Do you remember when he held you down with a pillow over your face till you passed out?" She doesn't.

At seventy-eight the Alzheimer's has advanced. She is the only person he recognizes.

He has broken his hip. The hip has healed. But he can't walk. He's forgotten how. It's near the end.

She sits pressing herself into him as close as she can. She holds his hand firmly. She wills the closeness to direct her words to what shreds of memory he has left.

"I forgive you." She says. "Do you understand?"

"Yes," he says nodding, "I think I do!"

STEVEN LEWIS

Steven Lewis, Literary Ombudsman for Read650, is a columnist at *Talking Writing*, and a member of the Sarah Lawrence College Writing Institute faculty. A longtime freelancer, his work has been published in *The New York Times, The Washington Post, Christian Science Monitor, the Los Angeles Times, Ploughshares, Spirituality & Health* and others. Recent novels include *Take This, Loving Violet*, and *A Hard Rain*, all from Codhill Press, and Finishing Line Press published Steve's poetry chapbook, *If I Die Before You Wake*. His backlist includes *Zen and the Art of Fatherhood, The ABCs of Real Family Values, The Complete Guide for the Anxious Groom*, and *Fear and Loathing of Boca Raton (a Hippie's Guide to the New Sixties)*. He divides his time between his writing space in New Paltz, New York and Hatteras Island, North Carolina.

THE RUINATION OF EVERYTHING

Steven Lewis

1945. June sometime. My late parents, who I trust must have loved each other in unobserved ways, are conjoined in some form of awkward carnal embrace, and I am conceived—a miracle of sorts, this being ten years after their first child, the prince, was born and eight years after their last child, the princess, had, by all accounts ended their mutual affections and their child-bearing lives. Perhaps it was a celebration of the World War coming to its end? My mother's birthday present? An "accident" after one too many Old Fashioneds with the Sussmans?

I don't know. But nine months later, I'm pretty sure my arrival at 135-18 77th Avenue in Flushing was cheered as if I was the new family puppy.

And so from early on, as I peered out the window of our garden apartment and saw my big brother escaping down the street with a Louisville Slugger over his shoulder, big mitt slung through

21

the barrel, I was not in the least forlorn that he said I couldn't tag along. I just figured he had better plans for me. Ice cream from the Bungalow Bar? Maybe Ebbets Field?

And later, after we had moved to the 'burbs, whenever my big sister Marj's teenage friends from Mineola High (rolled Levi's, thick white cotton socks, red Keds) cooed over me as if I was cute as a beagle, I understood that I was as cute as a beagle.

So ... picture calendar pages in 1940s movies flipping up in the wind and suddenly it's more than six decades later—and our mother has just passed away, leaving us senior citizen orphans. My brother and sister, hale and hearty into their 70s, are still around— and, all evidence to the contrary, I'm still the baby of the family.

As we three siblings are meeting to discuss funeral arrangements I detect something akin to mild annoyance from my older brother, something I have never noticed before. Is that a scowl? A sneer? I don't know.

I look over at my sister to check. Her smile lets me know I'm still cute as a beagle, albeit a 420 year old beagle. Maybe it's just indigestion.

But then it happens again a week later when we get together to discuss the complicated logistics of legal probate in New Jersey. There it is, that scowl. And I thought I was wagging my tail in the most charming of ways.

So I check with my sister once again: still a beagle.

But like a tiny flea bite that overtakes all other matters in a life full of grace, I can't stop scratching. It nags at me back home in the

Hudson Valley, drives me to tail chasing distraction as I teach a class on sibling rivalry in King Lear. Could he have had indigestion for a whole week? Maybe I should call him and suggest a colonoscopy.

So the next time we meet, I whisper to my sister Marj, who was always a second mother to me — and sometimes a first — "I think John's mad at me."

Then I snort as if that is the most absurd thing I've said in years, waiting for her to assure me in her most motherly fashion that it simply isn't possible.

But Marj glances over at me with clouds of pity in her eyes, as if ... I am as dumb as a beagle. As if it might indeed be time to put the little pooch down.

And after a pause, with what appears to be a smile squiggling across her face, she says, "Steve ... John's been furious with you since the moment you were born. You ruined everything."

JULIE EVANS

Julie Evans is a massage therapist, mentor, healer and writer. A contributing writer and columnist for *Healthy You* magazine, Julie can transform pain and loss into a launching pad for wellness–on the page, on a walk through the woods, and on the massage table. Other publications she has written for include *Pulse Magazine* and *Fictionique*. Julie's 2016 memoir, *Joy Road,* documents the story of her coming through the fires of rejection, addiction and redemption. Her current writing project reveals recipes for hope and healing and is entitled *Visits with Vera.*

THE LAST TIME

Julie Evans

The day of my dad's funeral, the three of us girls were sitting in my childhood bedroom, a room I really wasn't ready to leave, and we were having a talk. I was seventeen years old and freaking out that my two older sisters, Cyndi and Beverly, were taking over. For the last year, since Mom had died, I had been the one who took care of Dad as he was dying and neither sister even came home.

Well, to be fair, this really wasn't Beverly's home. She was twenty years older than me and had lived in Colorado and Malibu and Mexico when I was growing up. But Cyndi was only five years older and her room used to be just down the hall from mine. Mom and Dad gave her the bedroom over the garage so she couldn't sneak out her window. Little did they know how many times I had slid out that window.

Even though Bevy didn't live with us, she was hip and smart and I always knew she'd be there for me. When she'd visit I was her assistant, patiently ripping lettuce so as not to bruise it with a knife, or grating cheeses for her show-stopping enchiladas. She loved me—that I knew for sure. So as she sat next to me on the floor of my closet with my clothes hanging overhead, telling me what was going to happen, I was speechless.

She probably just didn't realize how much I'd just been through. I'd taken care of Daddy at home for the last six months. I carried him to the bathroom and wiped him had learned how to flush out his feeding tube and IV's. She probably just didn't understand how scared I was and how much I needed her. I thought she'd want me to move to Mexico and live with her.

And what was Cyndi doing looking through my dresser drawers? What was happening? And it hit me that this was the last time. It was the last time I'd be in this bedroom; the last time we'd be together as a family.

I had no words, and when I stood my legs felt weak and shaky. All the pride I'd felt in doing such a good job taking care of both Mom and Dad throughout my stormy life seemed like nothing. I tried to push all the love I had for everything into a safe place. Cyndi smiled as I left the room and Bevy just kept talking.

Four days later my oldest sister, who always said she wished she had been my mother, sold the green velvet couch where I had set Dad up during the day so he could look out the big picture windows and stare at his rock gardens. She sold everything, kept the money, and went back home to her little village in Mexico.

Cyndi got married and moved to Chicago and then onto Africa. She came to see me once after I'd moved to New York but that was a mess. And Bevy … well, several years after our dad's funeral, when my dog died, I called my oldest sister, but she wouldn't talk to me.

It's been an entire lifetime since I wandered out of the bedroom the day of our father's funeral. Yet even today I hesitate and sometimes stumble when someone asks if I have siblings. Yes, I have two sisters who haven't been in my life for over forty years. The next question is one I can never answer. Why?

STEPHEN J. BROWN

Stephen J. Brown is a retired technology consultant and college administrator. After telling stories for fifty-odd years, he is finally getting around to writing some of them down, and was awarded the 2014 *Talking Writing* Prize for Flash Nonfiction for his piece, *"How Can I Miss You When You Won't Go Away?"*

BEAT THE REAPER

Stephen J. Brown

On Sunday, July 10 of last year, my sister-in-law Barbara phoned me. Near as I can recall, that had never happened before, not once in 30-some years of our in-lawfulness. As I considered her name on my Caller ID, it crossed my mind that she might be wanting to invite me to a celebration of my brother's seventieth birthday, some weeks away—but the darkness in me feared it was more likely she was calling to let me know he was dead.

Brother Rob's medical history is long and wretched. As a child, he was over-treated with X-rays for some now-forgotten inconsequential symptom and lost 40% of his hearing. He should have been dead at twenty-two, when he first contracted Hodgkin's Lymphoma. But experimental treatments had recently emerged, and, the docs said, they would "beat that sucker into remission," and they did—with massive debilitating chemo and months' more radiation. The Hodgkin's recurred twelve years later and dragged him through another six weeks of treatment hell, ending in a prognosis of "cautiously optimistic."

Then, two years ago, thirty medically uneventful years later, his chronic sore throat was diagnosed as base-of-tongue cancer—almost certainly attributable, he was told, to all that nasty radiation that had been meted out to him decades before. The newest surgical approaches were less disfiguring. But there were no guarantees.

The week before the robotic tongue surgery, he asked me to meet him for a late dinner in the city and I did. But I parked at a one-hour meter, and we talked only about our kids. Except for when I picked up the check and our eyes met accidentally and I said, "It isn't fair." And he said, "No, it isn't."

But even that horror he beat, with miraculous surgical art and craft, chemo, and yes, more radiation.

In contrast to my big brother, I had my tonsils removed when I was four, and chicken pox when I was six. Since then, I've been fine, pretty much. Occasional tests, no unmanageable results. Smoking, drinking, gorging on beef, no matter. Picture of health. Maybe that helps account for why, over the years, I missed it all. Every episode. I mean I knew that he was ill, even that he was mortally ill, but I simply didn't process the information. He was diagnosed; he was hospitalized; he was treated; he was recovered. I was oblivious.

Barbara was calling from the Level I Regional Trauma Center at Stony Brook University Hospital. This time, it wasn't illness. My brother, she reported, had fallen—fallen, that is, twenty feet off the upper deck of his vacation home in Sag Harbor, into a bramble where he lay for an hour until he was missed. He had been medevacked to the Trauma Intensive Care Unit. He had broken his scapula, eight ribs on one side, one rib on the other, twice fractured his pelvis, punctured his lung and broken his coccyx. They had surgically removed his ruptured spleen. He was, she declared without any apparent irony, lucky to be alive.

A visit could not be avoided. A week into his stay, Rob was chatty. He was positively jovial.

He had almost died—again—and simply would not let me in on it.

JOHN GREDLER

John Gredler, poet and memoirist, is a frequent contributor to 650 who's been writing in notebooks and journals for most of his adult life. He honed his craft at the Writing Institute at Sarah Lawrence College, Bella Villa Writers, 125, and the Terzo Piano Workshops. A recipient of the 2014 Kathryn Gurfein Fellowship from The Writing Institute at Sarah Lawrence College, John's work has been published in *Atticus Review, Fictionique, Narratively, Dan's Papers, Westchester Review,* and *Talking Writing.* John lives and writes in Tuckahoe, New York.

WITNESSES

John Gredler

But you asked me about my brother. I guess he got pretty bad as a teenager, I just never knew it. Didn't want to know. I'd come home from school and go straight upstairs to my room in the attic. Well, our room, I shared it with my sister Kathy. I'd read or listen to music or just stare at the ceiling. If I knew no one was around I'd still play with my horses. I kept them lined up on a shelf next to my bed.

I never thought I had anything in common with John but we both changed after Dad left. We kind of disappeared. Not so much Kathy and Michael, maybe because they were younger. John loved Dad too much I think.

I'm trying to remember a poem John wrote about the sunlight coming through my eyeglasses refracted onto the wall. He wrote it on the slanted ceiling above my bed.

Magic arrowheads of light
   gentle ellipses
      fading fast

I read it every night for a long time. He did things like that. I had a Polaroid tacked to the wall of the four of us in the back of Dad's Impala. One day I noticed written on the bottom, 'witnesses to the death of love.' I cried for the first time since Dad left.

The four of us were pretty close. We held together kind of like birds in a storm, but I was the one more on the outside. I tried hanging out with them but drinking made me sick. Smoking pot just made me paranoid.

I was the oldest but still only eleven when Dad left. When Mom told me he wasn't coming back she broke down. I was tall for my age, taller than her and she leaned on me while sobbing 'What am I going to do?' over and over. All I could do was stand there and try to hold her up as she slumped into me.

John and Kathy smoked. I hated it, they'd leave the ashtrays full of their stinking cigarette butts. I always complained but they just ignored me so I would hide the ashtrays under the couch.

When John sent me that letter years ago, "Making amends" he called it, for stealing my babysitting money, I was stunned. And a check for four hundred dollars. I told him I thought the painters had taken it, but did I?

He asked me why I never said anything, 'Didn't you tell Mom?' No, I never did. He said he stole it over time so he could buy pot,

'Didn't you notice your roll of cash was shrinking?'

Maybe I did notice and maybe I didn't care and maybe I made up the story of the painters stealing it so I wouldn't have to think of my brother stealing my money so he could get high. I really can't remember.

I didn't want his money but he insisted. It's strange I know but I felt bad, like I'd done something wrong. His birthday was coming up and he was moving to a new apartment. I took that money and bought him a good set of pots and pans from Macy's.

Then there was that other letter, the one I'd rather not talk about, the one he wrote to Dad to get him to pay for my wedding. The twenty-four page letter. Dad brought it to me looking like he hadn't slept, looking all wounded. I said I wouldn't read it but he left it in my apartment and I did read it after he was gone. I was sick for a week. All the stuff I had avoided all those years, it was all there.

ANN LEVIN

Ann Levin is a freelance writer and editor in New York City. She worked for The Associated Press (AP) for twenty years as a reporter and editor, most of the time based in Manhattan. Before that she reported for papers in Texas and San Diego. Since leaving the AP in 2009, she has worked as an editor for the United Nations Population Fund and Columbia University, written articles for the *AARP Bulletin* and other publications, and contributed book reviews to the AP. She lives on New York City's Upper East Side with her husband, Stan Honda, a photographer.

KODACHROME

Ann Levin

"Rachel," I yelled, "come see the movies!" But you refused. You sat in the living room while the rest of us crowded around Dad's old projector, watching Kodachrome films of us in the 1950s and '60s flicker on a wall in the study.

Later, I asked why you stayed away. "Because they make me feel exactly the way I did then—anxious and bewildered."

You? Anxious and bewildered? I thought that was me, the middle child, never sure which way to go. There was Janet, four years older: socially awkward, academic—but determined. And you, four years younger—exuberant, impulsive, even reckless. And beloved.

You were Mom's favorite—the golden girl. Home from prep school for the holidays, showing up at their parties in sheer, flowing dresses; wavy brown hair bouncing off your shoulders; brown eyes on fire.

Later, when they weren't looking, you'd change clothes and

slip out the back to ride around all night with Jerry and his friends, playing pool, getting high. I'd tag along, older sister in the back seat, smoke a little pot, wonder how you managed to make absolutely everybody fall in love with you.

It couldn't have been easy, being the fifth kid in eight years. By 1958, Mom and Dad were tired of diapers, ready for new adventures.

They were happy to let the housekeeper take you home for the weekend to her little house on the outskirts of town. She fed you pierogis, stuffed cabbage—dishes we never ate at home—and I often wondered if the time you spent with her family made it easier, somehow, for you to be in the world.

You also had to deal with Howard, six years older, who teased you without mercy when you were a little girl. About being fat and hairy, which bothered you so much you used Dad's razor to shave off the golden down on your baby face.

The summer that you turned twelve, you went on that wilderness survival program in Wyoming. You came back thin as a willow, knowing things you were too young to know.

You told me you smoked hash one night in the middle of the forest. Looking up, you saw the trees, silent and forbidding. Beyond that, specks of stars, remote, inaccessible. You realized nature is indifferent, offering no consolation.

That fall, you were the only child at home. I was calling Mom and Dad every Sunday from prep school, weeping, lonely, homesick. It was then you resolved never to burden them with your troubles.

Recently I found some snapshots of your wedding, circa 1984.

You'd already been fired from your first job for drinking. You were lifting weights, hanging out with a rough crowd. You had the body of a Terminator, a haircut like Grace Jones, eyes glazed from Ecstasy.

Mom and Dad never knew the extent of the alcohol, the drugs—not until you wrecked a car, your marriage, got arrested, almost died.

How many years did it take to get sober? Mom says eighteen; I think it's more like twenty-five. I often wonder how else it might have been. But you rarely indulge in analysis or blame.

Those home movies you wouldn't watch? They don't offer any clues. Mom and Dad look so young and happy; they seem to be taking such good care of us.

Here we are in the backyard in late autumn, with Grandma and the aunts, the low, golden light casting shadows across the bluish lawn.

There we are at the shore, a month before your first birthday.

I'm standing near the lifeguard pole, squinting into the white sun, clinging to Dad's leg. You're in a blue-and-white ruffled bathing suit and diapers, crawling like a sand crab directly into the crashing sea.

.

JACKIE MERCURIO

Jackie Mercurio lives with her husband, five children, and black Lab in New York. She is an author, editor, and writing workshop teacher. Her work has appeared in many publications including *Good Housekeeping, The Washington Post, Woman's Day, Ploughshares Writing Series, Literary Mama,* and others. She earned a graduate writing degree from New York University in 1997, was awarded the Sarah Lawrence Kathryn Gurfein Fellowship Honorable Mention in 2012, and was named Winner of the *Good Housekeeping* Memoir Contest in 2014. Most recently, she was featured in the 2016 New York City cast of *Listen to Your Mother*.

CONNECTED

Jackie Mercurio

My three older sisters and I studied ballet from Mrs. Little, a former Radio City Rockette who lived in our neighborhood. She offered dance lessons in her basement, wearing shiny maroon v-neck leotards and smelling like Aqua Net, her hair dyed red and pinned up like Lucille Ball.

Her studio had floor-to-ceiling mirrors, and on the wall hung two framed photographs of a younger Mrs. Little on the stage at Radio City Music Hall. In one photo, she is in the famous kick line, her face bright and smiling, her toe pointed up, her arms around her fellow Rockettes. In the other, she is in a line of the well-known toy soldiers, their faces in profile, their arms at their sides, about to fall like dominoes. I loved how their red uniform jackets matched the red circles on their cheeks and how—although it was only a still image—my mind played it like a video, how the lady-troops fell slowly into each other, one on top of the other, like their bones had gone soft and their bodies collapsed, toppled, or rather melted into each other for support.

Because I was just eleven, Mrs. Little taught my teenage sisters separately from me. I'd watch their class from the dim stairwell, sitting on a step, my feet in black flat ballets. I'd see Fran, Tina, and Maria standing at the barre in pretty pink pointe shoes, with satin ribbons laced up their calves. They were so, so beautiful—so perfect—their arched backs, their long necks, their graceful hands.

Every now and then, I'd catch their eyes and smile. Sometimes they'd smile back, sometimes they'd make a funny face. Later on they'd take off their pointe shoes, and tell me, "It's harder than it looks." They'd show me their swollen red feet, their bruised toes.

And wasn't that always the case in life? When you see something beautiful, something perfect, there's usually some suffering behind it. I've never forgotten their perfect beauty—or their swollen feet, those bruised toes. And without realizing it, my sisters have repeated this lesson to me throughout my life. I have watched them earn degrees—for teaching, dentistry, and law—but not without the accompaniment of books sprawled on our dining room table, their weekends spent cramming for tests. I've seen each of them get married, but not without the suffering that comes from dating bad boyfriends and going through heartbreaks, learning the complications of relationships, and the painful work it takes to make a marriage last, or not last. I've also watched them hold their newborns, but not without understanding the emotional swings of pregnancy, the growing fatter, the suffering of labor pains, all of which brought those perfect babies—my nephews and nieces—into their arms.

Watching my sisters was like having a cheat sheet on life—like I got to see the answers before I actually found the answers myself. I'd observe and learn and rely on them for advice—especially when it was my turn to have a first boyfriend, to marry a man, to give birth to a child.

Many decades ago, in Mrs. Little's basement studio, my sisters and I would pretend to be toy soldiers. We'd line up. We'd lock arms. And one by one, beginning with me—the baby sister—we'd fall. Into each other.

Even today, after all these years, long after I left the ballet barre behind to go to college, to marry the man of my dreams, to birth my five children, my sisters are still the ones I rely on, the ones I collapse on, with interlocked arms, forever connected. Through life, like dominoes, we fall.

EDWARD McCANN

Edward McCann is an award winning writer/producer and the founder and editor of *Read650*, celebrating the spoken word with live events in New York City and throughout the tri-state area. A long-time contributing editor to *Country Living*, his features and essays have been published in many literary journals, anthologies, and national magazines, including *Better Homes & Gardens, Good Housekeeping, The Irish Echo, The Sun,* and others. His essay, "Pregnant Again," was selected for the anthology, *Listen To Your Mother*, published by Penguin, and he's recently completed a memoir about the search for his missing nephew. He lives and writes in a pastoral spot about eighty miles north of New York City, and is at work on a collection of essays about life in the Hudson Valley.

ROTTEN LITTLE LIARS

Edward McCann

It's 1970, and I am almost seven years old. My sister Mary, ten years older, has beautiful, glossy brown hair long enough for her to sit on. There are six of us, but Mary teaches me to swim, pulls me on the sled, and takes me to Harvey's for French fries with gravy. She even teaches me how to brush my teeth, laughing when I mistakenly swallow the foamy rinse water.

Mary's bedroom is my favorite place in the house, and it's filled with interesting things like straw covered Chianti bottles with drippy candles, and a hanging mobile made from wire coat hangers. She has psychedelic posters and sketchbooks, a guitar, and a record player, and sometimes we snuggle up together on the bed to watch *Laugh-In* on her very own little black and white television. Tacked up near the ceiling and slowly making its way around the room is a long garland of chain she's made from hundreds of aluminum pop-tops. It grows, like a living, creeping vine, and I bring home every pop-top I can find — offerings for my beloved.

Mary's word is law, and the law is clear about not entering her bedroom without an invitation and to absolutely NEVER enter her room when she isn't there. Sometimes she secures herself inside — and me outside — with a hook and eye latch. The linoleum feels cool against my cheek when I plead my case through the gap between the door and the floor, begging to be allowed in. Staying in Mary's good graces is paramount, because the best part of my world is the entrée into hers.

My older brother Jimmy is nine, and we're lying on our bellies at opposite ends of the long upstairs hallway scooting Matchbox cars back and forth along strips of orange plastic racetrack when the heavy front door slams. Mary's home from school. "Comin' through!" she says a moment later as she steps over me in her sandals and frayed bell bottoms, disappearing into her bedroom. A second later, she's back in the hallway with a 45 rpm record in her hand, demanding to know, "Which one of you was in my room?"

Jim and I both sputter denials. "Okay — someone moved my record. I know where I left it, and it was moved, and one of you is a liar." Suspicious of each other, Jim and I again profess our innocence before we begin accusing each other. Haltingly, under interrogation, Jim finally "admits" that he saw me go into Mary's room earlier that day. I'm so outraged by his lie that I respond with my own, insisting I saw HIM go in there. Not only that, but I saw him take something, too, and hide it in his room.

"You liar," Jimmy squeals, punching me in the chest. "You're a stinking liar!"

"Alright," Mary interrupts. "We'll find out which one of you is lying right now. Come in here."

We follow Mary into her room, where she holds up a book she says is a bible. Obeying her commands, we place our hands on it, each in turn repeating an oath she made up on the spot. Still, we continue lying, adding new details. We then watch in awe as Mary sprinkles talcum powder on the record, scrutinizing it for fingerprints. "Hold out your hands," she demands.

We're standing there before our sister, two little dummies with our palms up, when Mom appears in the doorway carrying a stack of folded laundry. "What's going on here?"

"Somebody came in my room and moved my record, and one of them is lying about who did it."

Mom sets the laundry on the end of Mary's bed. "I moved that record this morning when I gathered up your collection of water glasses to take downstairs. Why can't you bring your glass down in the morning instead of taking a new one upstairs every night?"

We're off the hook. Jimmy and I drop our hands to our hips and glare at our sister. Jim wants an apology, but his demand prompts only a single, bitter, big-sister laugh: "Ha! I don't have to apologize to either one of you because you're still a couple of Rotten. Little. Liars."

ACKNOWLEDGMENTS

In addition to the contributors to this volume, we thank Nancy Manocherian's the cell, which supported 650 at its inception. A twenty-first century salon in the heart of New York City, their mission is to support the arts and incubate new works, and the cell made its beautiful performance space available to Read650 as we were finding our way. The cell: To mine the mind, pierce the heart, and awaken the soul.
TheCellTheatre.org

Thanks to Patricia Dunn and The Writing Institute at Sarah Lawrence College for your encouragement, support, and for the steady stream of good writers you send our way. The Writing Institute helps writers in all genres progress and grow in their craft, and welcomes them all into a very supportive community.
SarahLawrence.edu

Artists Without Walls was created to inspire, uplift, and unite people and communities of diverse cultures through the pursuit of artistic achievement, and has supported and encouraged 650 from its beginnings. Artists Without Walls: No Limits. No Walls. No Boundaries.
ArtistsWithoutWalls.com

READ650.COM

INFO @READ650.COM
FACEBOOK.COM/READ650

www.ingramcontent.com/pod-product-compliance
Lightning Source LLC
Chambersburg PA
CBHW072045170626
46811CB00008B/3170